My Life Science Library

Animal Architects

Lisa J. Amstutz

Rourke Educational Media
A Division of Carson Dellosa Education
rourkeeducationalmedia.com

ROURKE'S
SCHOOL to HOME
CONNECTIONS

BEFORE AND DURING READING ACTIVITIES

Before Reading: *Building Background Knowledge and Vocabulary*

Building background knowledge can help children process new information and build upon what they already know. Before reading a book, it is important to tap into what children already know about the topic. This will help them develop their vocabulary and increase their reading comprehension.

Questions and Activities to Build Background Knowledge:

1. Look at the front cover of the book and read the title. What do you think this book will be about?
2. What do you already know about this topic?
3. Take a book walk and skim the pages. Look at the table of contents, photographs, captions, and bold words. Did these text features give you any information or predictions about what you will read in this book?

Vocabulary: *Vocabulary Is Key to Reading Comprehension*

Use the following directions to prompt a conversation about each word.

- Read the vocabulary words.
- What comes to mind when you see each word?
- What do you think each word means?

Vocabulary Words:

- *architects*
- *dam*
- *predators*
- *protect*

During Reading: *Reading for Meaning and Understanding*

To achieve deep comprehension of a book, children are encouraged to use close reading strategies. During reading, it is important to have children stop and make connections. These connections result in deeper analysis and understanding of a book.

Close Reading a Text

During reading, have children stop and talk about the following:

- Any confusing parts
- Any unknown words
- Text to text, text to self, text to world connections
- The main idea in each chapter or heading

Encourage children to use context clues to determine the meaning of any unknown words. These strategies will help children learn to analyze the text more thoroughly as they read.

When you are finished reading this book, turn to the last page for an **After Reading Activity**.

Table of Contents

Busy Builders

Architects draw plans.

They help build homes and bridges. Some animals build things too!

Home Sweet Home

Chirp, chirp! Birds build nests.

Nests keep their eggs safe.

Chimps build soft, warm nests.

They sleep high in trees.

Look! This nest is made of bubbles!

A fish will lay its eggs here. The bubbles will **protect** the eggs.

A beaver cuts down trees. It builds a **dam**.

The dam forms a pond.

Now the beaver makes a lodge.

There it is safe from **predators**.

lodge

Some ants build mounds.

They lay eggs in the mound. They store food there too.

Meal Time

A spider builds a web. The silk is sticky.

Bugs get stuck in the web. The spider eats them.

Bees make a comb. The comb holds honey for the bees to eat.

The comb holds bee eggs too. It keeps them safe.

Photo Glossary

architects (AHR-ki-tekts): People who design buildings and supervise the way they are built.

dam (dam): A wall across a stream or river that holds back water.

predators (PRED-uh-turz): Animals that live by hunting and eating other animals.

protect (pruh-TEKT): To keep something safe from harm.

Build a Nest

Try building a nest of your own! Follow the steps below or come up with your own design.

Supplies

twigs
mud
soft materials such as leaves, moss, grass, or yarn

Directions

1. Weave twigs together to form a nest.
2. Coat the outside of the nest with mud. Smooth it out.
3. Let the mud dry.
4. Now give your nest a soft lining.

Index

About the Author

Lisa J. Amstutz is the author of more than 100 children's books. She loves learning about science and sharing fun facts with kids. Lisa lives on a small farm with her family, two goats, a flock of chickens, and a dog named Daisy.

After Reading Activity

Go to a park or walk around your neighborhood with an adult. Can you find any structures built by animals? If so, take a closer look. Try to guess what kinds of animals built them.

Library of Congress PCN Data

Animal Architects / Lisa J. Amstutz
(My Life Science Library)
ISBN 978-1-73161-506-0 (hard cover)(alk. paper)
ISBN 978-1-73161-313-4 (soft cover)
ISBN 978-1-73161-611-1 (e-Book)
ISBN 978-1-73161-716-3 (e-Pub)
Library of Congress Control Number: 2019932049

Rourke Educational Media
Printed in the United States of America,
North Mankato, Minnesota

www.rourkeeducationalmedia.com

Edited by: Kim Thompson
Produced by Blue Door Education for Rourke Educational Media.
Cover and interior design by: Nicola Stratford

Photo Credits: Cover logo: frog © Eric Phol, test tube © Sergey Lazarev, cover tab art © siridhata, cover photo © Enrique Aguirre, cover title art © itsmokko, page background art © Zaie; page 4 © Popartic, page 5 © fotoNino; page 6 © Mark Bridger, page 7 © Vishnevskiy Vasily; page 8 © Sergey Uryadnikov, page 9 © COULANGES; page 10 © anapat duangngoen, page 11 © By mnoor; page 12 © Piotr Kamionka, page 13 © Adwo; page 15 © ian Tessier; page 16 © David William Taylor, page 17 © Beneda Miroslav; page 18 © boyphare, page 19 © Cathy Keifer; page 20 © FaRinPh, page 21 © David Shih All images from Shutterstock.com